The Hard Life And Musings Of A Young Adult

A collection of poems about life and stuff

Trinity Adams

Made with ❤ on the BookLeaf Publishing Platform
www.bookleafpub.in
www.bookleafpub.com

Dedication

This book is dedicated to all the people who struggled and are struggling to make their own way in life. To all the people who don't have it easy, to those who are lost, scared and confused. To those who are told they'll never make it but still try anyways. To those that ate told they're too much. To those who are told they'll never be enough. To those who have to leave everything and everyone behind to better themselves even if they didn't want to. To those who don't have the support they need to make hard choices and have to make them on their own.

I see you. You're valid and you're not alone. I'm always in your corner :)

Preface

Truthfully I didn't know I'd be doing this. I've always been writing since I learned to read and hold a pencil. I've made comics and did fanfic commissions in school for a little extra money.

Writing has always been personal to me. An act of rebellion. Speaking my truth and making others happy. To show others that there is a light at the end of the tunnel when the rest of the world doesn't want you to.

It's high time I spread that hope elsewhere. I hope y'all can enjoy

Acknowledgements

I would like to thank my amazing significant other Danny for always being there for me and making me a better person. For giving me the courage and support to do this.

I would like to thank my family. Even though they weren't the best they still made me who I am today. They have given me inspiration for these poems and the ability to make my own choices and do what was best for me.

I would like to thank my friends. Y'all know who you are :). I wouldn't be here today if it wasn't for you. All of you. The ones I've known since 2nd, 4th grade, to the ones I've met in middle and high school. To the ones I met at Jobcorps. To the ones I met in my new adult life. To the Og friend group I know life gets in the way many of us are different people than we were in middle school. A lot of us had falling outs with each other. But if it wasn't for you I wouldn't be here today. You all taught me what love, home, family, acceptance and belonging was supposed to be. You kept me going when I couldn't go on for myself. You gave me the inspiration for life and to keep on going to see where it leads to. You guys brought out the best in me and paved the way for others.

To the ones I met at Jobcorps. Yall taught me that no matter who you are or where you came from you it's never too late to start better yourself and your life. No matter the race or creed we're all human beings just trying to do better. Definitely taught me some humility and to be more understanding and patient with others.

To the ones I met in my new adult life. Whether I've known you for a day/month/year. You all taught me that it does get better. Maybe not immediately but it certainly does. As long as you make the time for what's important.

To all the people who hate me be it from our school days or in the average everyday life. I don't wish you any harm and I do hope you get the best in life. Just so you know I'm doing this out of spite.

To bookleafpublishing thank you for this amazing opportunity and I couldn't have done it without you!

1. Birth

I was brought into the world.
So small and innocent
I had to come out through force.
I guess that paved the road for what life was going to be like for me.

2. Neglect

I'm sorry I was a difficult child.

Maybe that's why I was ignored out of punishment.

I'm sorry for trying to be good.

Maybe that's why I was easier to ignore.

The trouble with young parents is that they're so focused on themselves and their own lives that they barely notice anything around them.

Like a race horse with a blinder on only focusing on whats ahead of them.

The never ending race of life.

Interaction conditional based on worth.

How useful I could be or what I could do for them.

Conversation was a transaction.

A hefty price to pay

Leaving me in debt.

Hours upon hours in the hellscape that was Loneliness.

You know what they say thats the price you pay for true freedom.

I always thought I would be okay with that.

Until I overdraw.

See the trouble with older parents is that you grow older with them.

So they think that you're okay because you can take care

of yourself now.

Failing to realize that's what you've been doing all along.

3. Childhood

I miss my childhood.
It was the best of times.
And it was the worst of times.
I miss who I used to be.
I miss the pure unadulterated freedom I had when I
wasn't with my parents
I miss childhood summers.
I miss being idealistic and believing thats how the world
works.
I miss who I thought people were.
But all that is in the past.
Its true what they say
Nothing good can ever last.

4. Friends

Friends are an essential part of life.
They bring out the best and help you in strife.
Strength in numbers
Always fun slumbers.
Life is hard when you feel alone
But when you have someone in your corner
Life becomes more bearable when you have someone to
call home.
United we stand. Divided we fall.
As seasons change
Sometimes friends become estranged.
But to the ginger girl
Who always gave my life a whirl.
To the blonde who is always random
You were the one who taught me fandoms.
To the girl who was hard to pull.
You're 90% of my impulse control.
To the woman I met at work
Who knows how to pull the cork.
You guys brought out the best in me.
And I hope one day life will set you free.

5. My Father's Praise

Father knows best

At least that's what they say.

There was once a time where I loved that man more than anything in this life.

I didn't understand why he hated me so.

There was once a time where I would have done anything for him. Anything to hear him say that he was proud of me that I was worthy to be called his. I would have killed for him and I did. I killed myself and any semblance of what I could have been. I've broken every part of me until there was nothing left.

And what did that get me?

Nothing.

My father liked to drink a lot.

And it was those times where he was softer and kinder to me.

They say drunken words are sober thoughts.

I thought it meant something.

I thought that if I could crack the code on what to do to earn those praises sober I could open the vault to the love he supposedly had for me.

I never did. They never lasted long.

We all have our vices and addictions.

And when those moments came back up just like my

father downing the bottle I would always drink the
sweet poison of his words like I would never see water
again and become drunk on his praise.

6. The Rebellious Teen

have never done what I was told.
I never have and never will.
Especially since your true self is hard to hold.
I refuse to conform.
To stay quiet and follow the norm.
I refuse to listen to people who don't have my best
interests.
To the weak willed, indecisive and shitty people.
I refuse to apologize for who I am.
I will march to the beat of my own drum
And blaze my own path to glory
If you don't like it suck it up or leave and get out of my
way.
Or to those that feel the same stay.

7. My Mother's Hatred and My Father's Arrogance

I know my parents tried with what they had.
I'm upset that they didn't try anything new or try harder.
I'll never understand why my mother hated herself more than she loved her own children.
Always taking what she could get and putting herself in dangerous situations with her firstborn on board.
I'll never understand why she was so selfish.
Laughing at my father's boulders of insults and abuse as if they didn't hurt us.
She never once stood up for us.
I'll never understand why my father thought that being right and the best all the time was more important than understanding his children.
I'll never understand why his arrogance was more important to him than anything else in the world.
Unfortunately I have the worse aspects of both parents combined.
Suppose it runs in the family.

8. Rebirth

Some say that rebirth is a dramatic transformation.
That wasn't the case for me.
It started out small.
Something clicked inside of my head saying no more.
I started focusing on things I could control.
Then gradually everything pieced itself back together
like a long destroyed puzzle.
Maybe not complete like it once was but there was still a
whole picture.
Sometimes rebirth happens slowly bit by bit.
Eventually I began to rediscover myself. I've gained new
thoughts and beliefs and expanded on what I had.
I became stronger and better.
I'd give anything to go back to that self discovery.
Sometimes rebirth happens slowly then all at once.

9. To the Ginger Girl

This one goes out to the one who has always been there
for me since day one.
From a chance seating on the bus I knew I just had to
have you in my life forever.
You saved me that fateful day
After a promise of returning the next day.
I didn't have the heart to tell you the truth.
You taught me what hope, home, love, family and
acceptance were.
You have saved me more than you know.
Even though we were girls together you've helped me
grow into the woman I am today.
And for that I thank you
My best friend.

10. Choices

the hurricane there is quiet for just a moment.
I had a brief moment of clarity once upon a time.
I was given a choice
Either stay at home with people who didn't care
Or be out on my own.
I've been asking for a second chance at life since I was
12.
And here it was presented to me like a gift.
The million dollar question was
Was I willing to leave behind everything and everyone I
knew behind including the old me for a small chance at
freedom into the unknown?
It stumped me for a minute.
I didn't want to leave those that were dependent on me.
But i knew if I stayed where I was any longer there
wouldn't be a me to take care of others.
How can I if I can't take care of myself?
They say in order to get a life you have to give a life.
So I made my choice
I left and haven't looked back since.

11. So This is What Freedom is Like

The first steps by myself were scary
Leaving everyone and everything I knew behind.
I knew it was for the best of course.
I knew that things couldn't be worse.
I knew freedom was a tantalizing thing.
Something out of reach.
No one told me how exhilarating freedom would be.
The first thing I did was jump on the bed.
Then I bought a jar of Nutella with my own money and
ate it straight up.
Yes being on my own was scary and hard
But it was oh so worth it.
Sometimes freedom tastes like the wind's back
Sometimes freedom tastes like a jar of Nutella.

12. To the Best Roommate in the World

This one goes out to the best roommate in the world.
The one who was so shy and dark at first.
As you broke out of your shell I saw the light that shone
through the cracks.
You taught me that there is virtue in being kind and
professional.
You taught me how to play computer games.
You got me into rp.
You showed me that there was another way of living
through hardships. That I didn't have to live hateful and
bitter. That I could have a better life and heal.
You helped shaped the adult I would become once I left.
And for that I thank you and hope you'll continue to
stand by me and live your adult life with me.

13. Culinary And Food

The moment I chose this career was the moment that I knew I was meant to do this for life.
It was the one thing I was good at without destroying anything.
I thrived in the midst of chaos.
I love food.
Food is the language of the universe and soul.
It was the one thing that my father and I bonded over when we weren't at each other's throats.
I say if your problems can't be talked out over food then they can't be solved.
Food doesn't solve everything but it does make things better.
Food is what brings people closer together after all.
After a hard day of getting your ass kicked on the line and surviving with your crew it just brings a sense of comradery.
There's nothing else like it.

14. Love

There are many definitions of Love.
No two loves are the same.
And certainly not plain.
Love is a skill
Love is something you have to train to have
Love is a discipline
Love is not something you have it's something you have
to create for yourself
Love is hard but you must pick it up again
Love is a shield and use to defend
Love is a an end in itself and a means to an end.

15. To the Blonde Girl

This one goes out to the blonde girl I knew long ago.
I met in math class passing notes back and forth.
Who taught me about fandoms.
Who gave me interests and hobbies.
Who taught how to roleplay.
Who taught me not to take myself and life too seriously.
Who taught me mischief and fun
And if this poem finds you, I hope you'll be around in
the long run.

16. Danny

This one goes out to my one true love.
You've helped me in more ways than one.
You saved my heart; you've helped me heal.
You make me want to be better.
Our love isn't easy.
But it's a choice I'll continue to make without a doubt.
If loves a labor I'll slave to the end.
I would go to the ends of the earth and hell and back if
that means I can crawl home to fall in your arms.
Before you came along, my life was blue.
And with this, I hope you know my love is true and
there's nothing that I wouldn't do for you

17. To My New Friend in the Here and Now

This one goes out to one of my friends in the here and now.
I'm glad I met you when I did.
You taught me that it's okay to be myself as an adult
Being an adult wasn't as bad as I thought it was.
That it was okay to enjoy and live life and go at my own pace.
I have so much fun hanging out with you
And I hope that you'll continue to be in my adult life

18. Advice

Let me tell you what I wish I'd known many years ago.
You are not the center of the universe.
Everyone is too selfish and wrapped up in their own
lives to worry about what you're doing.
It doesn't matter what others say and think about you as
long as you know the truth about yourself.
And if they don't like it then they can either suck it up
or leave
And fuck right off with the rest.

19. Mothers Apologies

My mother said I'm sorry.
I thought I'd be happy.
It's everything I ever wanted.
I wanted her to admit she was wrong and just as human
as everyone else.
Then why don't I feel any different?
Instead, I felt more anger and confusion.
Why was that so hard to admit when I was a child and
needed it most?
That you wanted to be treated like the almighty and all-
knowing when you couldn't even meet the expectations
of one and then got mad when I pointed out you didn't
and called you human.
When I was right all along.
They saw mother is the name for god on the lips and
hearts of all children.
Well, you're no god to me.
Now, I'm left with more questions than answers
I have so many questions to ask you
I'm left more confused than ever.

20. Of Little Brothers and Protective Older Siblings

The day my little brother was born, I felt something shift when I held him.

Something clicked in place and awakened in me.

That "Oh" "Oh" moment.

I knew I had been changed forever.

As time passed, I won't lie, I began to hate him.

He was treated better than me.

The stark difference was like night and day.

Highlighting that I was never considered anyones

Even my mother chose him and her husband over me.

Eventually, I didn't blame her. I began to pick him over me and anything else.

He made me see just how young I was. How young he was when I was his age.

I chose to protect him from the evil man in the house. To protect him from me so he wouldn't end up like me.

He has such a bright future ahead of him that I didn't see it for myself at the time. I wanted to do everything possible to give him what I didn't have.

I'm sorry that I left, and I hope one day he'll understand It was for the best.

21. The Adult Life

The adult life wasn't what I expected.
Truthfully, I didn't know what to expect.
I always thought it was meant to be full of misery, dull
and crippling loneliness.
Since that's what I saw all around me growing up.
I wanted to do everything in my power to stop that
process
Including binging and starving so I could remain
malnourished and not go through the puberty process.
Anything to prevent myself from becoming like the
adults I saw around me
Anything to avoid becoming a woman and make my
father's rage at my existence less.
You know, I cried on my 18th birthday.
Waiting to magically feel like an adult was supposed to
happen when you hit that magical number.
Nothing happened.
I was left confused.
Eventually, I realized no one knew how to be an adult;
they were just faking it.
So, I realized it was okay to make my own way of being
an adult.
Taking baby steps like a fawn learning to walk for the
first time.

Slowly but gradually, I'm getting the hang of this adult life.